Tires? They're Optional

Richard Reale

ISBN 10: 1535548045
ISBN 13: 9781535548045

Table of Contents

INTRODUCTION

A free 1940 Humber Bicycle, just sitting and waiting. It will be a fitting final vehicle after a lifetime of transportation modes I enjoyed owning…generally. Fitting, I say, because the memory of my first bike remains as vivid today as when I first rode it more than sixty years ago. I was three or four when my brother and cousins, laughing a *lot*, sat me atop a big kid's bike and pushed me down the grassy hill. I got about halfway down before toppling over. The adrenaline and exhilaration were never to be forgotten. Although my feet were fully twelve inches from the pedals, I was hooked! Two or three years later I could balance using a girl's bike, but it took a lot of scraped knees and elbows before that happened.

It seemed like forever before I received my own two-wheeler, a fat-tired Columbia. I was about nine, and three-speed English bikes were just becoming the craze. I couldn't wait or think of much else. Finally, after a lot of good fourth grade grades, Mom bought me a cheap Sears and Roebuck catalogue three-speed French bike. It was junk! I had so many flat tires I stopped trying to fix them. I rode an entire summer on the rims. Starting wasn't bad if I went easy, but once I got up some speed, stopping was the fun part. Eventually the spokes started to fall out, and shortly thereafter the wheels would collapse. More scraped knees and elbows, passengers included. I wonder if their additional weight had anything to do with the collapsing wheel syndrome.

About then, Dad bought a new 1955 Buick, and a new experience consumed me: making a two-ton object travel from point A to point B. I was big for eleven, and actually drove well, compared to Dad. For the next five years I chauffeured my parents just about everywhere. I actually drove down Broadway in New York City at age twelve. Although it wasn't legal, we were probably safer with me driving instead of Dad. He was about sixty at the time and just didn't care to turn his head much. Parking by ear was the norm. Getting his license was an interesting event, as the story goes. Pop showed up just before closing, and the inspector asked if he could drive, to which he replied, "Sure," to which the inspector replied, "Good, here's your license. My wife has supper on the table."

Being born in 1896, in Sicily, he probably didn't see a car till he was about fifteen. Even as an officer in the Italian Army during WWI, he rode a horse. His life was interesting, to say the least. After the war he earned a Ph.D. in economics from the University of Rome, and was involved with politics and government in Italy. Shortly thereafter, he came to the USA and founded a bank. It folded in 1929 as a result of the stock market crash. Several restaurant businesses consumed the rest of his working life; a few were very profitable, but all were hard on family life. Also, it's not the best example to set when a patriarch's philosophy is: "I'd rather have five dollars in my pocket and owe a thousand, than have nothing and owe nothing." Growing up around that thinking doubtless contributed to my chronic and adventuresome risk-taking tendencies.

Getting back to me driving the new Buick at age twelve -- I guess it just didn't seem like a big deal to Pop, compared to all that he had seen and done. For example: he had royalty as friends in college, he knew Mussolini, he met Puccini in Paris at the opening night of his opera *La Bohème.* He also achieved the status of "Cavaliere" in Italy, which many regard as on par with English knighthood. He is the one who really should have written a book.

Although we got along very well despite a half-century generation gap, I miss Mom more. Sadly, cancer claimed her when I was just a teen.

Back to foolish adventures.

At age fourteen, I left the state with an eighteen-year-old friend in his mother's car. We were gone two weeks and my parents didn't know where I was, but I did have a friend let them know I was okay. Although it was fun at the time, now that I'm a parent I realize how thoughtless I was, and wish I could turn back the clock. I spent those days driving his mom's '49 Chevy around New Hampshire while he stayed with a girlfriend. We slept next to a gas station that got robbed. We were awakened by the local police and taken to the station. Now remember our situation: very little money, two weeks sleeping in the car, bathing in the ocean, out of state, and me a minor. I had a friend's birth certificate to show I was eighteen. I really didn't look like him, so they asked my name and I told them. Still doubting, they asked my middle name. Uh-oh! How's this for chance? I was sure his middle name wasn't Alphonse, which mine is, so I said Francis, which is my confirmation name. Nothing was said. A few more questions and I was handed back the birth certificate. Sure enough, Friend's middle name was Francis! After mug shots, fingerprints, and about six hours, we were let go. Talk about luck and avoiding *big* trouble. The next story's ending was slightly different.

Also at age fourteen, I bought my first car, a 1950 Ford, for ten bucks. It was light blue with many flat black primed areas. Of course I wanted to customize it; I just didn't have any money or a clue about what to do. A friend and I relieved a car dealership of one 1958 Impala, which at the time was about six months old. He took the motor for his old Chevy, and I took the seats for my Ford. After pulling the engine, we were transporting it in the trunk of my unregistered, bizarre-looking Ford, when upon making a left turn, it fell out. Now it was in the middle of the highway. With infinite stupidity I stayed, directing traffic around the motor while others went for more help to lift the motor back into the trunk.

Unbelievably we did it and were back on the road, me riding in the trunk (lid open) with the motor.

As fate would have it, another friend's father was pulling out of a side street as we passed. He began asking questions, for which there were no sane answers. That's when things started to fall apart and we got caught. I was a juvenile and managed to avoid incarceration. My friend was older and was given the choice of jail or service. He became a very good soldier and I, although still adventurous, quieted down considerably. A final piece to that story happened about 6 months later when I persuaded my friend "Tar", (nicknamed that because his dad was a roofer always working with molten asphalt) to drive my now, NOT im-pounded, (but still unregistered) Ford home. We almost made it. Near the end we hit a rough patch of road and things changed *really* fast. Because the Impala seats went back to the Impala, we were sitting on barrels. The shimmy was so bad we fell off the barrels, aaaaaaaand crashed.

The investigating officer kept asking what we were driving, refusing to believe that we really were driving the car without seats or registration and a smashed windshield. Ah yes, the good old days. Fortunately, Dad was well liked in town, and after several court appearances, Tar got off relatively unscathed. I didn't say a word when Dad called the junk yard to come for my first car.

A year or so later, the day came for me to become legal and take my driver's test. I failed. The reason, per the inspector: I was "too confident." Not surprising, as I had probably logged 20,000 miles on Dad's Buick over the past five years. I got my license a month later and proceeded to lose it a month after that. I think a three-month suspension was automatic for a teenager caught speeding. Being clocked at 106 may also have been a contributing factor.

Maybe six months later I bought my first legally drivable vehicle, a 1931 Chevrolet half-ton pickup for $150. It looked cool and ran, but defined the word "heap." Ben Edson's garage sold drain oil for ten cents a quart. I figured it was much better than no oil. On the other hand, the tires were not much better than no tires. You couldn't find new tires that size. Even if they were available, they were unaffordable. Any I found were cheap or free, but very old and dryrotted. If they held air at all, it wasn't for very long.

One Friday evening both rear tires' lives ended. Four spares in the truck's bed were already flat. Having had a beer or two and being no stranger to riding on rims, I kept driving, just slower, in search of the opposite sex, as usual. My built-in speed slowing safety device did raise a few eyebrows, especially when one of the shredding tires got caught in its covering fender and ripped it off the body. Now at this stage, the adjective "heap" was more like flattery. It was quite a sight, its silvery rims sparking along downtown on a Friday night, cruise night! Well after all, Meriden was known at the time as the "Silver City" of the world due to the many flatware factories. I was just adding a new dimension.

Around 1:00 or 2:00 a.m., it was time to call it a night. I had to travel a longer, roundabout way home because I could not make the steep hill, as *no* traction was the order of the evening. (Even the old mechanical type brakes worked pretty well if the wheels had tires; otherwise, you just hoped and prayed it would stop before crashing into whatever.) Meanwhile, sparking up Allen Avenue, I saw many lights at the next intersection. Thinking there was only a small chance the lights were from police cars, I proceeded to get up as much speed as I could, on rims (maybe 30-35 mph). I was wrong about the lights. They were coming from police cars: five, to be exact. It was too late to stop. As I sparked by, the corner of my eye detected the inevitable, a flashing gumball atop a cop car, heading after me. I pulled over, and a flashlight-wielding policeman approached in what appeared to be disbelief, while eyeing my chariot.

"License and registration please," he requested, to which I replied, "Well, sir, I have them, somewhere."

Luckily it was Officer Bailey. After he saw who I was, he said while shaking his head, "Reale, you can't do this. You must have rubber on the road. I don't care if the tires are flat."

He held the light as I put on different wheels with flat tires; then he followed me home. Those were the days.

(Who could resist such a cutie, driving around in an antique pickup with no back tires?)

I could never afford anything but maypops -- that is to say, "may pop at any time." I wouldn't bet any of those old tires would ever hold air, except once. This particular time I gambled on a tire I sold to the Hawk (nicknamed that because he could recover a fumbled football faster than anybody else in the world). I bet him it would hold air for thirty days. He had a '57 J2 Olds that could spin the tires, it seemed, forever. He was really intent on winning the bet and getting his five bucks back. On day twenty-nine when the tires were amazingly still holding air, he went for broke. That Olds had so much torque he ripped the center right out of the wheel, tire still intact, holding air. He came to me upset but laughing, knowing that I hadn't guaranteed the wheel.

Back to the pickup -- another tidbit. The passenger's seat just sat unsecured atop the gas tank. One day, after school, with about half a dozen passengers in cab and bed, I rounded a sharp corner and the passenger's door flew open. The seat, with Cal on it, slid across the tank and out the open door onto the road. He was still sitting on the seat, but it was now sliding on its metal framework at about 20 mph. No injuries, no seat damage, never even spilled a drop of his soda! That was Cal; you just had to know him!

Probably the most memorable experience was when Emerling (nicknamed that because it was his mother's maiden name, and we just liked it), and I were delivering papers one morning about 3 a.m. in that1931 Chevy pickup truck. It was January and cold! There were 275 papers in the bed, and the wind started to kick up, blowing some away. I turned to look in the bed and of course, having my hand on the steering wheel, it turned also, right into a 1958 Chevy station wagon, ripping its driver's side doors completely off. It was another friend's car, and he was delivering nearly a thousand papers. I can still hear him stuttering, "Wwwwwwwwwwwhat am I gggggggggggggggggoing to dddddddo, it's cccccccccold!"

My insurance paid the claim and of course raised my rates, which I couldn't pay. From then till I got married seven years later, I drove with no insurance. Probably the only thing more stupid and unthinking was passing someone on a blind curve to win a race. I cringe thinking about what could have happened. I thank the Lord especially in regard to that incident of stupidity. There were others, but even innocent contributing factors can alter one's judgment. Examples are of course alcohol, drugs, sleep deprivation, even anger. Anything that affects one's judgment, even in the slightest, is like playing a scary game of "Russian Roulette" with yourself, and *others*! Driving is our way of life and no one expects to crash, but the numbers are staggering. Please be aware and careful.

The mid-fifties to the mid-sixties was a golden age in Meriden for being a teenager: blue suede shoes, duck tail or flattop haircuts, cars and trucks cruising downtown on Friday night with no mufflers, just "straight pipes." We ice skated at Hubbard Park with the first music of Rock and Roll legends. With Billy Rudolph in his father's 1951 Ford, I remember going to the State Theater in Hartford to see Chuck Berry, Jerry Lee Lewis, and Little Richard in concert, of course all staged by the famous promoter, Alan Freed. That was 1958, when cool cars were lowered at the rear, and had loud dual exhausts. Also a partial or fully primed ride somehow added to the mystique of "Who is that guy and what mill lurks under his hood?" Incidentally, that flat black primered retro look is back, especially with those who are restoring and recreating Hot Rod nostalgia.

In the early sixties, John DeLorean of DeLorean car fame, spearheaded efforts to build a reasonably priced, intermediate sized "fast car". He was a V.P. at GM and got the job done, culminating in 1964 with the introduction of a racy new Pontiac G.T.O. It was short for Gran Tourismo Omologatto, and marked what most considered the birth of the "Muscle Car Era". Prior to that factory fast cars in my town were somewhat rare and unusual. Ford and Chevy had already given the public a taste of power with supercharging and fuel injection respectively but sparingly, based on limited demand, especially with teens, as we were usually moneyless. Some kids were good backyard mechanics and provided us with speed entertainment at the local dragstrip. For most of us however "Fast Cars" were cars that we just drove fast, and unsafely. The latter because of no seatbelts, no radial tires, no disc brakes, sloppy suspensions and foolish risk taking, in which category I was a perfect fit. I even fancied myself as a drag strip racer up until the strip rules mandated all entered cars must have a scatter shield welded around the flywheel and transmission. Sadly, the fifty dollar installation fee simply eliminated all hopes of ever competing in a sanctioned drag race, but unsanctioned events of speed and unsafety were common. Pop's Buick and I stupidly defined those reckless activities, so naturally that lowly 188 horsepower, 2 ton load became notoriously a "Fast Car", and occasionally challenged. One such instance where "Fast" was tested, became legend.

It was against "Whip" Haras and his dad's 1955 Chevy station wagon which sported the new optional V8 engine. Whip, proudly but humbly, always said it was pretty quick, which never sat well with "Tar" Mauri, a diehard Buick enthusiast. Whenever "fast car" talk was the subject of conversation, Tar's patented response was, and still is, " It'll be a close race, but the Buick will win.", which often led to the inevitable showdown.
Since Tar's dad's !953 Buick Roadmaster wasn't running anymore, ever, after he and six friends snapped a telephone pole in

half at 90 mph, my dad's '55 Buick was elected to test Whip's '55 Chevy. Probably the greatest testament for Buick wasn't speed, but strength, proved by the fact that no one was hurt in that unbelievable telephone pole crash!

We raced twice. Both times the wagon won.........up to about 85, at which time Tar riding with me yelled "Now Rick Now!" which meant shift from low to drive, and the Buick pulled ahead for the win. I thought for sure my transmission would meet the blacktop in a thousand smoking oil soaked pieces. To this day Whip is still mad, Tar still smiles, and the wins are still legend. How could anyone think different after looking at dad's Buick on the cover of this "Literary Masterpiece." ☺

Haras was a gracious loser, but certain events are never forgotten. That memory I bet influenced some of his future car purchases. One particularly notable machine was a 1958 Ford retired police car. THAT was fast! Additionally using black market aviation jet fuel made it unbeatable until it also ruined the interceptor engine. More than a half century later, Whip Haras still drives a collector series G.T.O., daily!

Now for some other cars in my life;

I won't attempt a chronological history of my vehicles, but will touch on many, as each has a story, and most are worth remembering. I'll list the makes alphabetically, generally remembering the oldest and progressing to the newest owned.

I'll begin with Buicks, although I did price a brand-new Amphicar around 1966. It wouldn't have been a bad investment in retrospect, except I didn't have $27, let alone the $2700 price tag.

BUICK

A 1951 Special. This was more my speed, and quite possibly a record-setting achievement, but at least a personal best, and a peek into the past of our country's economic disasters.

Imagine buying a decent car, registering it, driving it from Connecticut to Maryland and back, including gas, oil, and tolls, for a total expenditure of thirty-four bucks. Granted, the registration was only temporary ($2) and there was some gas already in the tank, and the car was only $10. Compare that to the cost of anything today; it's sickening. Yet we spend incomprehensible dollars trying to bail out poorly run businesses. Two days before we voted to bail out GM and Chrysler, I sent the following letter to the local newspaper editor. It was a culmination of my thoughts not just about the auto industry, but moreover lots of US decisions in the past that have led us to owe *twenty thousand dollars* every *second* just for *interest* on the national debt!

"The American auto industry has a giant effect on the US economy and its people. It can't be fixed in the sense of "business as usual" -- that is to say, overproducing and being kept afloat by incentives and Madison Avenue advertising. People can buy only so many new cars, no matter how good the deals are and how much credit is available.

In 1923 National Geographic Magazine ran a twenty-page article on the American auto industry. Its basic conclusion was that America had reached the automobile saturation point and could not sustain further similar production rates. Since then we have produced, who knows, maybe 100 times as many vehicles? Well, we are saturated, and money poured into GM and Chrysler will be wasted in the long run if its purpose is to keep the industry as we know it. Focus needs to be on wartime strategy, so to speak – on research, development, and production of items that will protect and sustain America, not tens of millions of vehicles every year, perpetuating the 'Throw Away Society.'"

Too bad it fell on deaf ears; instead, we wasted how many *billions*? At least now, American car companies are producing what we needed twenty years ago. Better late than never, I guess.

One hundred ten years ago, America had no taxes and no debt. Let's keep praising the economists and politicians; they must know what they're doing. After all, look at their Ph.D. and MBA degrees. I'm not against higher education -- I just think some of it tends to erase common sense.

Back to my car stories and some smiles.

A 1952 Roadmaster. Wish I had it now. Really nice, and a tank! Sold to a friend 'cause he liked it so much.

A 1954 Roadmaster. Every car has a story; some are pretty interesting. This one I bought specifically because it was the oldest car on the lot from the oldest Buick dealer in the country. To me it was pretty neat, and worth buying just for that distinction. It was a good car that I gave to Dad, and he drove it for two years before a noisy wrist-pin finally let go. I should have fixed it. I didn't, but definitely got my $60 worth out of the car.

Next a myriad of '55 Buicks, the most significant being the one Dad bought new, in which I learned to drive, and finally inherited. Around 1963 when it needed brakes, two tires and a battery, I tried to sell it for $25. Oh yes, I forgot to mention it had considerable rust and I had used it in a basic sandlot version of Demolition Derby. It emerged not unscathed, but victorious and driveable.

Anyway, back to the sale.

I had a buyer for $15. I said, "Okay, but I keep the radio." The buyer wanted the radio. I was stubborn, no deal. I was also sentimental and proceeded to restore the car. The "restoration" consisted of two new tires, a battery, and brake pads which I installed backwards. The total cost was $55. Although it needed new brake drums, to keep the cost down I had the original drums cut 40 thousandths over the legal limit.

Now adventurous, and accompanied by two equally nutty friends and a combined pool of about $325, we decided to drive cross-country and back. You may remember I did tend to drive fast, and what better excuse than trying to visit Tar, 3000 miles away, and returning within the week? We told our parents we were visiting friends in Cape Cod, about four hours from home. Seven days later we arrived back home. It was the same day Gormley's parents received notice of a speeding ticket gotten by him in Arizona. We all thought there'd be hell to pay, but actually everybody was happy we were home.

In fact, Gormley was the one to tell me new cars couldn't do what I did on Route 66. I remained at over 100 mph for over an hour in a rotted, banged-up car that had the original antifreeze, hoses, and belts. I guess Studebaker wanted to prove a new car could do that, because that same year they introduced their new supercharged Avanti model with a picture and the caption "Coast to Coast in 48 Hours." All in all we made our destination cross-country in fifty-eight hours, but that included two speeding tickets, one of which I had to go to the police station at 3 a.m. to forfeit bond and pay the $34 fine. It also included getting lost in St. Louis for two hours, going to church and mass Sunday morning, and stopping somewhere for an oil change and service. I estimate we lost at least ten hours total. So that was forty-eight hours or fewer of driving time in a car that I couldn't sell for fifteen bucks.

It weighed at least 4000 pounds, had 188 horsepower, and got as much as 20 mpg on the highway. It even had a race with a 1957 Buick which had 300 horsepower. It was a dead heat at 115. The three fellas in the '57 got the biggest kick out of my awful-looking car keeping up with them. On one stretch of old Route 66 we covered 100 miles in 55 minutes. Although it was insane to do such a thing in that car, it was safer than hitting 100 mph down Broadway in NYC one particular 4:00 a.m., not being chased or inebriated, but just wanting to do it.

The entire next year I drove the car to and from college, putting maybe another 15,000 miles on the odometer. Somehow I came across a dual quad setup and managed to install said speed equipment which actually looked great, but really only poured gas into the engine without increasing its speed. I believe it contributed to – and may have been the direct cause of – a burnt valve. I reinstalled the original two-barrel carb and still got 15 mpg.

A year later, the other two nuts and I decided to drive to Acapulco. Trying to amass enough money to do this, I reasoned the $45 it would cost for a valve job would automatically eliminate any possibility of driving to the southern tip of Mexico. So with infinite stupidity and winning-the-lottery luck, we departed on a 9000-mile odyssey, burnt valve and all, not to mention a front end so bad I ran snow tires, figuring they would last longer. As we entered Mexico and customs through Laredo, Texas, a young boy, maybe nine or ten years old, ran into the car and rolled across the hood and off the other side onto the ground. He got up, looked at the car shaking his head, and walked away. Even at that young age he knew the scam was useless and there was no money to be had in that Buick.

We were gone three weeks, taking turns driving and sleeping, except for a five-day treat in Acapulco. We had an efficiency room for three in a brand-new motel. We paid $30 total for five days right on the water. We also stayed one night in Mexico City for $2. Remember, it was 1964, and the most common taxi was a Model A Ford. It was an interesting, adventurous trip. One experience in particular remains vivid. We had a flat, and luckily had a spare. We were in the mountains, so who knows what would have happened if we'd had no spare. Anyway, we got back to the big city, Acapulco, and went to its biggest garage/gas station. There were easily a hundred locals there, employed or not, but all busy. One took my wheel and flat tire, crossed the street, and waited on the opposite corner. By and by a bus stopped when flagged down by the man entrusted with the repair of my flat. To my surprise and delight and admiration, the fixer placed the tire in front of the bus's rear wheel and signaled for the driver to proceed. The primitive process was done to break the bead in order to patch the tire's tube. It took three buses to break the tire's bead. Wow! Before you could say *ándale*, we were back to carrying a workable spare, but not before filling the tank with government-regulated 79 octane fuel called Mexolina.

The car was running terribly. Duh. I blamed the fuel, which seemed logical, never even considering the fact that it had a burnt valve. We made it back the thousand miles to the US. I then filled the tank with 104 octane Sunoco. We drove about fifty miles, using about half a tank of fuel, and felt no change in the way the car was running. I pulled into a garage and explained the situation. Remember, it was 1964 and gas station employees knew stuff and helped! The mechanic opened the hood and said, "Hmmmm – it could be this stupid chrome air cleaner." It was clogged solid from the dusty conditions we encountered throughout Mexico. It had been a big mistake to remove the original oil-bath air cleaner, no matter how cool the chrome cover looked.

En route, we bought some Mexican pottery. Nice, except for the massive urn. We stopped once on the Pennsylvania Turnpike to rest, putting the urn outside because it took up so much room. An hour later we were back driving. Five miles down the road, we realized the urn was left behind. Although it was 6:00 a.m. with no traffic, I got a reckless driving ticket for backing down the turnpike. I woke up the justice of the peace to pay the fine, and after seeing us and the car, he wanted to add a vagrancy charge. He couldn't because we still had twelve bucks left. That was plenty to get home, as gas was only about twenty-four cents a gallon.

During our odyssey to Mexico and back, I was fortunate to avoid much adversity. My passengers however, did not fare so well. Gormley, pictured on the cover in the middle, occasionally was less than enamoured with the voyage. He was most concerned with cleanliness, which after five days of 100 plus temperatures, travelling in a car with no air conditioning , and the odors coming from white t-shirts turned yellow with sweat, needless to say made him a sometimes grouch. During our pit stops for gas, we could count on him scrubbing his face with a constant companion, Clearasil soap. He really was the smart one. I guess 50 plus years later, his being an authority on Nuclear Missiles has proved me right.

Now imagine one evening trying to get a little shut eye at a pit stop, after about 15 minutes and already in deep sleep from exhaustion, Mazzone and I awaken to Gormley's yelling and swinging frantically trying to kill a spider, or night bug, or whatever which seemed the size of a large tarantula, crawling on his chest. Poor Gormley, he was having a tough time of it, although I think getting somewhat used to the discomfort, especially after the vulcher incident.

There we were, lost somewhere in the badlands of sweltering Mexico, Gormley at the wheel, Mazzone and I trying to sleep as we had already been about 5 days and nights travelling constantly. Again we were wakened by Gormley's frantic voice.

Now readers, picture if you can still doing about 70, the vulcher he had just hit, stuck in the side vent window, head and neck flailing about, inches away from our pilot's head. Luckily the impact killed it, but dead or alive that was an ugly bird.

Mazzone's memories I'm sure were vivid also, especially the one where he got deathly sick in Acapulco from either the water or the food. He was so afraid of Montezuma's Revenge that he constantly switched our food so as to insure we would all get sick if one of us somehow got the bug. Needless to say, he was the only one who got sick. We finally got a doctor for him after he lost at least 10 pounds in one day. Not good for someone who is already pretty thin. The good doctor gave him a shot and some medicine and told him to stay in bed for 5 days. Well that could not happen because it would have cost another 10 dollars each for 5 more days of lodging. We left the next morning convincing him he be fine on the car's back seat for 5 days. He was obliging and a bit gullible, a fact often verified. I once convinced him, he with perfect vision and me legally blind without glasses, to try on my contact lenses. I reasoned and said "Just imagine how much better you could see with my contact lenses, especially since you have perfect vision already." Well that sounded logical to me and him, the two stooges. Of course neither lens fit, and both got lodged somewhere in his eye sockets. I quickly and profusely invoked the

Lord's help, which He did eventually, and miraculously, but not before I conjured up many sickening scenarios.

Still digressing from Mexico, another close call was when I asked him to pilot a car I was going to tow to the top of a steep hill. About midway up, Detective Roberts passed us coming from the opposite direction. He saw our illegal, unsafe towing attempt, and quickly looked the other way. He knew our automotive endeavors were always insane. A fact proven minutes later when near the top, the car I was towing became disconnected. It and Mazzone at the wheel were now gaining speed Backwards! Oh, and without brakes! Luckily, he veered left, went through a fence and down a bank, landing in a field and amazingly unhurt, proving the Lord does tend to protect fools. He probably has this scene on video file, and watches when He needs a laugh. Such fun, those days of almost catastrophe. Now back to our travels.

I have lots of other memories of that Mexico trip, but enough said. We made it home and that evening a tie-rod broke as we simply stopped for a red light. The Buick's final year was spent beside my dad's diner, providing housing for two homeless friends, one of whom had served in both world wars. This was a noble final service for a car that literally gave its all.

Another venerable Buick was a '55 Roadmaster. It was a nice solid low mileage car purchased for $75. I think it was so cheap because it needed paint. One memorable evening I took a shortcut using a new and unopened road. It was dark, as the streetlights hadn't been installed yet, and I didn't see a telephone pole lying across the road. Luckily I was going slow when the car and the pole met -- maybe 10 to 15 mph. In an instant I was looking at the sky, then again at the road. The sequence was followed by a horrendous noise coming from below the floorboards. Next, the rear of the car rose up six or eight inches, and quickly back to level again. The four-holer, as the big-body Buicks were known, never missed a beat.

I stopped to investigate the cause. We'd run over the telephone pole, which had been lying across the road as a barrier. All of the Roadmaster's vitals were protected by being above its massive frame. Only the differential housing was partially below the frame, hence the rear raised as the car, rolling on its frame rails atop the pole, reached the differential housing. The momentum never stopped and the car was finally free and back on its wheels, with no damage! Try to do that with any modern car today. To that add the fact that the pole, approximately 16" in diameter, was sitting atop 8" curbs on either side of the road. What a car!

Next, a '56 low mileage four-door hardtop. It was another four-holer and also under $100. I used it for a year or so, then sold it to a friend in need. He drove it for years and maybe another 100,000 miles. One evening, which is vividly remembered to this day by my passenger, Bill Reardon, we were returning from a weekend at a car show in Hershey, PA. It was 2:00 or 3:00 a.m., and we still had 100 miles to go. You recall that I had been known to speed. Bill, older and much wiser, even in slumber knew I was really moving. He awoke to glance at the speedometer, which would show a red square for each 10 mph. Twelve was the maximum showable, and all twelve were visible.

He exclaimed, "RICK!"

Thinking quicker than normal for me and not wanting to appear the fool I was, I faked waking up and thanked him for being so alert. To this day, whenever we are together the story of how he saved our lives is told. I'm sure if he reads this book, he'll know for sure he was riding with a fool. Even though I was totally awake, he may very well have saved our lives.

Next, a '57 super convertible. This is possibly the car I miss the most and one that rivals the '51, pricewise. This was a great car that I bought from a dealer for $25. I suspect the price was so low because the transmission gave out within a week or two. A restored one like it sold at auction for $195,000. Anyway, the fix was $200 and I was in business. I drove it throughout Canada on my honeymoon in 1967. Although the speedometer maxed out at 120 mph, I believe it would do an honest 130 with a feeling of relative security. (If Bill is reading this, I bet he's thankful we didn't use the convert.)

The best story here, by far, is as follows: one evening while riding around in a smallish snowstorm, I came across an eighteen-wheeler spinning his wheels a little way into a long hill. He wasn't going anywhere very soon. I stopped and offered to pull him up the hill, a moderate grade about a quarter of a mile long. He laughed and said I would pull the rear end right out of that Buick. He would have been right, I'm sure, except he could spin his tires, and the Buick's wheels also spun, but afforded enough traction and pulling power due to new studded snow tires. As both vehicles slowly spun the drive wheels, we began moving, and after about fifteen minutes we reached the top. No overheating, no damage, just amazement on his part and pride on mine.

At the top of Hubbard Park hill, I stopped, unhooked the chain, and said, "Have a nice evening." As I drove away he was still shaking his head, and I bet if he's still alive, he tells that story often. That's a picture

really wish I had, but at least here's one of the car and me.

Next, a 1960 rust-free LeSabre two-door hardtop. Although I never took possession, it's a good story and relates to a cross-country eBay purchase. It was an old but good Suburban from California, and the seller was kind enough to deliver it to Lake Tahoe where I was enjoying a family vacation. My plan was to drive it home to Connecticut after our vacation. Those plans changed completely and instantly. The following recounts why.

Being a skater of old, I did bring a battle-scarred pair of racer skates loaned by my good friend and clergyman, Dr. Robert Maloney. It was 1957 all over again for me, except for a few slight differences. It was fifty years later and we were at a famous ski resort that was having an exhibition given by a group of recent Olympians. There were probably 10,000 people in attendance, and needless to say it was a fashion show of both outfits and state of the art equipment. I didn't stand out *too* much in dungarees, a leather jacket with the collar turned up, and old racing skates slung over my shoulder. The only thing I lacked was enough hair to comb into a ducktail. By the way people were looking at me, I'm sure they were thinking, *Who **is** that guy*? It was great, especially knowing my outfit was the same as it would have been fifty years earlier.

I was feeling pretty good on the ice, and while never averse to pushing the envelope, I started some moves that generally resulted in more than just the skate blades coming into contact with the ice. Inevitably I lost it, but this time there was a problem I hadn't factored into my fall. Due to two very bad wrists, I couldn't protect myself while falling. I went down hard and sustained a concussion, resulting in dizziness for about five weeks. I never saw such a look of fear on my daughter's face as when she heard my head hit the ice. No one has a more concerned, caring child.

Needless to say, driving the newly acquired Suburban back cross-country was out of the question. Luckily, my daughter and her friend Rob drove it back to Santa Monica, and the rest of us flew back to Connecticut. Four months later I returned to the West Coast to fetch my Suburban. En route, I visited my old friend Pete in Arizona. After several days with him, reminiscing and imbibing, I was not anxious to drive 2700 miles. His neighbor agreed to store the orphaned Suburban in her back yard for a while. Finally, here's where the nice 1960 Buick LeSabre coupe enters the picture. It also lived behind her house. It was also for sale, and offered to me for a grand. Instead, I took pictures and put it on eBay. It sold for $3400. I gave her $2400 and used the other $1000 to have a transporter deliver the Suburban to Connecticut. It was a win-win situation for everybody, and also a good example of how car nuttiness can weave a web of interesting events and situations.

Next was a 1964 Electra. It was Dad's, but I drove it a lot. I arranged the deal through the local Buick dealer who said he could get a World's Fair display car. Although worried about the $120 monthly payment, Dad said okay because it was such a great deal. It had a few hundred miles on it but still carried the new car warranty. We had no idea what style Electra would arrive, as the good deal was first come first served, and you took what you got. One day shortly thereafter while driving past the Buick dealership, I spotted a very special car just coming off the carrier. Later that day, Dad got a call saying the car had arrived. Lo and behold, the really nice one was Dad's. It was a two-door with the 425 big

block. It was super plush but also fast. The paint job was super rare, black with a copper roof. I was in college and spoiled, and stupid for trading it in for a new Power Wagon in 1967. Anyway, good memories with it -- courting my wife, etc.

Another rare and absolutely stunning Buick was bought from a very old friend who had bought it new. I loved this car from the day he brought it home from the showroom. It was a loaded '66 Wildcat convertible. Dark green, white top, black interior, factory mag wheels. Ted kept it really nice. He liked it when I gave him a big mounted bell. It was a first place trophy awarded at the Belltown antique car club's annual show in 2006. I sold it in 2008 to a collector from Chicago. I'm very happy knowing it is well taken care of, and appreciated.

Here's a good story about a 1974 Regal Colonnade coupe. I won an eBay auction for it, and it had 14,000 original miles. It had great color and eye appeal. Shortly thereafter I advertised it for sale, in hopes of turning a profit. A man saw it and sent me an e-mail inquiring about its background. Other than the fact that I had bought it from Pennsylvania, all I could tell him was the name on an old registration. He replied saying it was his wife's great-aunt's car and that she bought it new and the mileage was probably correct as she hardly ever drove it. The interesting part of the story was that she had a twin sister, and when they were toddlers, they and their family were denied passage on a ship bound for America on a transatlantic voyage, because the sister had a bad cold. Although this was a large problem, a few days later their feelings of inconvenience changed to extreme gratitude. Their voyage had been booked on the Titanic. The old story: when your time is up, it's up; when it's not, it's not.

I decided to keep the car, and did so for a few years. I finally sold it to an older gentleman in upstate New York. He loves it and I'm sure it is getting great care. I did keep an old registration which the original owner had signed. I think anything that even has a remote connection with that fateful voyage is worth saving, if only to remember and pay respects to all those lost lives.

Next, a 1977 Century Custom wagon. Really nice, pretty rare, and drove great. Unfortunately, my second son rendered it not worth fixing. Pictured before its demise.

My final, disappointing Buick was a 2000 supercharged Regal that I bought new. After six years and 60,000 miles the most I could get in trade was $4000. That translated to over $4500 per year to drive. Although new is nice, and it was quick, I deserved what I got. My automotive deals certainly run the gamut from great to terrible. Fortunately, the former is the majority.

CADILLAC

Although I'm not a Caddy guy, I have owned a few. The first was a 1929 LaSalle roadster bought for one Ben Franklin. The rumble seat was damaged but still usable, and great fun, especially going to high school football games, top down, with me wearing a big fur coat.

After storing it for the winter, I took it out for a ride in mid-April. Battery charged, coolant added, and off we went. It was 70 degrees, sunny and perfect. The coolant was water, as I thought it would never reach freezing again till the following year. (I bet you know where this is going.) Somehow that night, 15 degrees was fact. Also fact was that the cast iron heads of the big flathead V-8 opened up and looked like stuffed cabbages. Ah, the power of ice! Possibly the block was okay and damage confined only to the heads. Regardless, it was time to move on. I sold it to a man for thirty-five bucks. He said he wanted it only because it had two good tires. Such generosity. At the time, he had more than one Duesenberg undergoing restoration. I have since seen this car restored with an asking price in excess of $100,000. I have no complaints, since I had my fun, it probably needed an engine, and I lost only $65. Heck, I once bought a 1958 Caddy for $10 because I needed a battery and it had a good one. I took the battery, then junked the car. The only *slight* difference was that I didn't have multimillion-dollar cars being restored.

Another of my Cadillacs was a very nice 1954 Fleetwood. It achieved 21.7 mpg on a trip. I really should have kept that one. The last one, and more recent counterpart of that '54, is a 1991 Fleetwood Brougham. It is a low, low mileage, mint, always garaged, one-owner car. It seems, according to many, the 90-92 Broughams with the fuel injected 350 engine and true wire wheels represent the Holy Grail of the big and classy Fleetwoods. It is probably the best of an era, never to be duplicated, I'm sure. It's nice to own one.

CHEVROLET

These experiences began at age four. Mom, my brother, and I were walking out of church one Sunday morning when Dad met us in a brand-new Chevy Fleetmaster convertible. I remember Mom's words to Dad: "You JERK!" I'm sure they were tempered, as we were still on the church steps. He did spend more than he could afford when it came to cars.

At age six or seven, I remember the smell of smoldering leather as I burned the Ballantine Ale three-ring logo sign into the Chevy's door panels using the car's cigar lighter. I was lucky Dad didn't do the same thing to my butt. I was the baby, and spoiled. At ten, although I couldn't depress the clutch pedal and see through the windshield at the same time, I was allowed to try to drive in an open field. Adrenaline again! Shortly thereafter, the '48 was traded for the famous previously discussed '55 Buick.

The next Chevy, also previously mentioned, was the 1931 pickup. Then there was a really nice '51 two-door with dual exhaust pipes and glasspacks, a '55 convertible, '67 and '72 wagons, many Suburbans , and a new 2009 Silverado. I liked the wagons a lot; maybe that's why I've also owned seven Suburbans.

One lucky tire story is about the 1967 BelAire wagon. It was a nice clean car with an original 396 factory big block. At the same time I also had a 1951 Daimler Special Sports. It was an

English convertible with a custom "Barker Body." Only about 650 were made between 1950 and 1952.

Anyway, I sold it to a man a thousand miles away. I had no money, so I agreed to deliver the car just to make the deal happen, after he sent a $500 deposit. I used the money to rent a trailer and finance the trip.

My wife, three toddlers, and my eighty-year-old old dad set out with me in the wagon, pulling the trailer and car. Around 10:00 p.m. and about 150 miles into the trip, I stopped for fuel. As I was gassing up, the attendant asked me how far I was going.

I said, "About another 900 miles."

He replied matter-of-factly, "That's a stretch."

I said, "What do you mean?"

He said, "I don't think the tube popping out the side of your right rear tire will last another 9 feet, let alone 900 miles."

I'd say needing gas right then was a bit of luck. I changed the tire and proceeded with no spare. I think over the years I could have been a poster child for the phrase "Go with God."

Reaching our destination, I unloaded the car and went into the buyer's house to get the balance. I had about $10, and the sole of one of my shoes had half fallen off. Mind you, this was a really nice home. The owner also had a 1935 Lincoln convertible bought new by Clark Gable. It was Saturday evening and he gave me a check! Not wanting him to know I was broke, I left. I made it to my brother's house about 200 miles away. The next day I inspected the car and the rear tires were shot as a result of the trailer not tracking properly. I stayed a few days, was able to cash the $1500 check, and bought two new tires. When I got back home they were also shot, even towing the empty trailer.

The '72 wagon was also a good story. One day, my neighbor Patsy stopped me and said, "Rick, buy my sister's car."

Of course I said okay, sight unseen. It was a '72 Kingswood that I used for work for about five years. When my daughter finished college, she said she wanted to drive cross-country to California for her first job with Mattel as a toy designer. I let her take the twenty-three-year-old Kingswood. She called me from Ohio saying, "Dad, the car won't start." Right then I really questioned my judgment.

Having no inkling as to the problem, I blurted out, "Jiggle the battery cable."

A bit later she called and said, "We're on our way." Never another problem.

Being a parent of four driving teenagers may be the ultimate test for remaining calm. It seems "Going with God" -- or at least with Saint Christopher -- has been hereditary.

That Kingswood's factory green color caused the children to affectionately nickname it the "boogerwagon." Although it served Melissa well, she would have no part of using it anymore.

"Dad, a young professional girl in LA driving a giant old wagon? I don't think so." I told her she could be a trendsetter. I didn't even get a reply on that one. My wife and I visited her after a while. After it had been sitting in the basement of her parking garage for a year, I bought a battery for the Kingswood and it fired right up, and ran better than ever. I suggested driving it back cross-country. I figured it would be a fun adventure. Riiiiiiiiiiight. My wife was visibly upset just at the thought. I advertised the Kingswood and probably could have sold ten of them. I got more than the $500 I had paid six years earlier. The buyer was really happy, and it was off to a good home.

All my Chevy Suburbans have been good, including the one that got demolished in a my-fault accident. One evening I made an improper turn, and although I was going very slow, a crash happened. Both vehicles were demolished. Thank heaven no very serious injuries occurred. I was never so grateful as I was that night. I also became acutely aware that anything at all that affects one's reaction time -- be it alcohol, medication, drugs, even sleep deprivation -- could mean someone's life, or the lives of others. Lastly on the Chevy scene is a 2009 half-ton Silverado I got as a result of the "Cash for Clunkers" program. I bet most of the people who were against the program just didn't qualify. I feel the four billion spent did a lot of good and was a pittance compared to the Chrysler and GM bailout money squandered.

CHRYSLER

It was 1965 and I spotted a 1941 Chrysler Royal sitting on a used car lot. Naturally, I stopped. It did have some rust, but not bad, and totally acceptable for me. The price was fair at $125, but what really got my interest was that it had been traded by the original owner and had gone only 36,000 miles in 24 years. Done deal! Shortly after getting it home I removed the seat covers, which had obviously been installed in 1941, because to my surprise and good fortune the interior was virtually brand-new. That was special, but spectacular was the button-tufted, subtly striped broadcloth. I remember the rear seat curved at either end to cradle its occupants. I have a mint original 1941 Packard Clipper, and the interior is like new, but doesn't rival the sumptuous Chrysler's. It also had turn signals; the Packard doesn't. Also, I loved the way the speedometer needle gradually changed from amber to red the faster you went. In addition to its features, this '41 conjures up a great tire memory.

It was football season, and my town had a semi-pro football team called the "Meriden Shamrocks." On a whim, as always, four or five of us decided to go to an away night game in Maine, about 200 miles away. We left around noon in the '41 Royal. Too bad it wasn't a Type 41 Bugatti Royale. *That* would have been a *story*, as the six that were made all still exist, and are in the twenty *million*-dollar range.

Back to the story at hand, and reality. Perhaps midway down the highway, one of the tires no longer wanted to fulfill its function of holding air. Of course, no spare. Why would I ever want one of those? After all, I was only going 400 or 500 miles in a pre-war car with possibly the original tires. Had my passengers known about the no-spare situation, I'm sure they would still have been there. It was usually all good, regardless of what happened. We have lots of smiles, reminiscing. Anyway, back to the story; I pulled over to the roadside and for some unknown reason, I had a jack.

After removing the wheel, I proceeded to roll it back down the highway. There were no gas stations, but about half a mile back was a shopping center. I crossed the highway, and went over the guardrail and down a bank to the shopping center parking lot. Still no gas station, but there just happened to be a '54 Dodge parked, which also had fifteen-inch diameter wheels. Handily, the trunk was unlocked. Rationalizing is an amazing tool! Somehoooooooow, I reasoned the owner would really rather have a 1941 Chrysler wheel for a spare even if the tire was flat. With that, I hastily accommodated his imagined wish and gave him a most desirable Chrysler wheel (and flat), simultaneously relieving him of an air-holding Dodge spare. Sprightly I went, out the lot, up the bank, over the guardrail, and down the road to my three-wheeled Chrysler. As I was installing the fourth wheel, one of the car's card-playing occupants asked how I made out, to which I replied, "Not bad." Off we went for the rest of the trip, without a hitch. If it had been a Bugatti Royale, a good spare wheel and tire might not have appeared…as quickly.

The only other Chrysler was a 1963 New Yorker wagon, pretty rare -- big, heavy, and luxurious. It was Chrysler's counterpart to GM's Nomad, Fiesta, Caballero, and Safari. Its 413 engine was hearty and thirsty. Its rectangular steering wheel was novel and nice. Much too nice, in fact, to cut nearly in half as I did with an old Plymouth in hopes of simulating an airplane steering mechanism. (Trust me, you haven't lived until you're turning a corner with half a steering wheel, and forgot you did away with the other half!) Anyway, back to the wagon.

I remember my son John reading the car's name on the hood. He was about five, and he slowly said as he was pointing to each letter, "It's a C-A-R-S-L-E-R." He's forty now and really not a car person so to speak, despite his middle name being Packard, and ironically at one point having done four or five years as director of design innovation for arguably the most prolific auto manufacturer in history, Mattel's Hot Wheels.

Another memory is not of the event itself, but what happened afterward. My wife Sue has a wonderful memory of the New Yorker wagon stopping dead, in traffic. She, at 105 pounds and alone, pushed the 5000-pound car out of the traffic line! *Not* good! *Hell* to pay!

Lastly, I learned the art of anticipating where to park, in order to easily unpark, the reason being a broken reverse gear. That year was simply irreversible.

DODGE

Not much here except a 1951 half-ton panel truck which had seen better days, but was still cool. I never needed to dispose of drain oil from other vehicles, as I used it for the Dodge -- two to three quarts whenever I needed fuel. Once I used about ten quarts between fill-ups as a result of transporting shortened telephone poles about ninety miles. They hung out the back six feet or so, nearly touching the ground (that happens when 5000 pounds go into a half-ton truck). Even I couldn't believe the job was accomplished without incident from police or truck.

Next, and definitely at the other end of the spectrum, a very rare and desirable, super nice 1970 Coronet R/T. It was also an FC7 car with Chrysler's legendary magnum high performance 440 big block. FC7 was its color code, a high impact purple they called Plum Crazy. It was a very special car, but did have a few issues which, although minor, I chose not to fix and sold the car. I was probably still upset that it was misrepresented by being told over the phone that it had no rust and the chrome was perfect. The lesson: don't trust pictures and sellers' words when buying a vehicle, especially when big money is involved.

FORD

My first was the previously mentioned 1950 sedan. Remember the one I put Impala seats in, and then it had none?

There was another 1950 sedan. It was my friend Paul's daughter's car. It was excellent, to say nothing of the many memories I made with it at the drive-in movies. I still have an occasional Manhattan with Paul, discussing whatever. He's only ninety-eight. There was yet another 1950 sedan I bought with my good friend "Hawk" Mauri, "Tar's" younger brother., for ten bucks. We thought after stripping the parts we could sell them for a giant profit, optimistically 50 skins total on the high end, to split! I can't remember just how we managed to get the car on its side, but I guarantee it was not done safely. When accomplished, it looked like a beached whale, but we thought, while on its side, transmission and differential removal would be cake. That done, and after days of grime and scrapes, six of us pushed the hulk over to again be right side up.

Mrs. Mauri was fuming and regularly bellowed, "Get that garbage out of my yard FAST!" She always seemed to overreact when our inventiveness altered the curb appeal of their home. How silly I thought as we were forced to quickly remove the obstruction. After all that exhausting useless work with homemade, and/or, stone age tools, the junkyard got the car and all the stripped parts, because there were no buyers, or even TAKERS !

The following is an account of that particular fiasco. Enter innovation, and insanity:

We proceeded to jack up the Ford rear section about 4 feet, then backing my 1931 Chevy pickup to within 6 inches of the Ford hulk, we lashed the two gems together with a long chain tied around the still intact Ford bumper and two steel pry bars which we inserted vertically into the bed of the pickup. Reverse jacking the Ford left the two vehicles precariously connected. NOW of

course, we were totally ready to bring the Ford to the junkyard, which was closed, as it was Sunday evening. Although my visions are still clear, I won't attempt any illustrations. I will let you, the reader, conjure up those sights, either in the yard, or en route to the junkyard, with an obligatory flat tire of course, midway, with no spare.

What a spectacle! Think of two piles of scrap having sex, as they bounced and smashed into each other because the binding chain was so loose, and one driving wheel had an airless tire. Then NO, but now, I wish Officer Baily had witnessed that episode. Hopefully the Almighty has a video to keep us smiling for all eternity.

I've had several Ford trucks, including a Connecticut Light and Power bucket truck, and a new F150. Every one was good.

There was also a 1966 Fairlane GTA convertible with a 390 motor, which I bought in 1967, so it was almost new. I sold it two months later. It was exhilarating to drive and I was constantly being exhilarated, but my fuel bill was three times the normal amount. It was fire engine red, with a white top and interior. I wish I had that one back.

Lastly there was my 1957 T-Bird, which I bought from a friend. It was stunning in gunmetal gray. I kept it about twenty years and thoroughly enjoyed it and the people I met as a result of driving it. I sold it to a man who bought it for his wife. They drive, show, and enjoy the '57. No regrets, as I know it is appreciated and maintained. Thanks, Jim Dinunzio for your great help making it a win-win deal for all involved.

GMC

There was a rust-free 1978 I bought in California, and a 1961 one-ton pickup. I wish I had a picture of the pickup. It's a wonder I got any work, but it did have a good plow. The interesting story here is the connection with its previous owner. We met as a result of my interest in buying the truck. He had a sign repair and maintenance business. One day he called and asked me if I would look at a job. Basically he had taken the job, but didn't know how to do part of the sign, the reason being that it extended past the edge of the roof (about ten feet) into no-man's land, ten stories above the sidewalk. Being a former grade school teacher, I really didn't know anything about rigging or OSHA, or in this instance, sanity. I also had no clue and told him I would think about it, while really thinking I'd be a fool to attempt applying paint. I reasoned I shouldn't bother and he would never know my risky thoughts -- except I also thought of possible success. The danger and awaiting adrenaline rush masked the possibility of not surviving. So against sound judgment, I suggested we extend a 24' plank and apply rules of physics, like a see-saw. The heavier end obeys gravity and the lighter end defies gravity and stays in the air. Mike, being heavier, stayed on the roof end, and I literally walked the plank to paint the sign. Safety harness? What's that? I suspect it was a good thing I worked only one year teaching and influencing young minds in a fifth grade public school classroom.

JEEP and SIMILAR

There was a 1945 Army Jeep. It was lots of fun, with a look straight from *M*A*S*H**.

Then there were a couple of mid-1960s Land Cruisers that I used for plowing. They've really gotten popular among collectors today.

Lastly was a 1965 Nissan Patrol. I plowed with it for five years and made more than I paid for my home. I also used it for my work vehicle. Before its demise, the frame broke but was held together by a rear spring and reminded me of a Slinky. I wish I had a video of me plowing with the broken-frame Nissan Patrol.

I probably could write another book just on the snow-plowing adventures I had with my brother-in-law, Tom. A couple of tidbits are as follows:

It was the blizzard of '78 and after three days we were so exhausted we entered a vacant condo to sleep. It was so cold we pulled up the wall to wall carpet and rolled ourselves in it for warmth. Ahhh, sanitation plus.

Another time I heard on the CB radio, "Fire on Green 3, fire on Green 3." When I found Green 3 (a '56 International dump truck), Girard, who rode shotgun, was crawling out from under it holding a sleeve. It was the only part left of his jacket after he had wrapped it around the emergency brake, which had been left on, and the friction had caused it to ignite. Luckily it didn't reach the gas tank or a fuel line. From then on, Baird, one of our ace drivers, would always ask, "What will I be driving?" I don't think he liked Green 3, but it really didn't matter as all five of our plow trucks were junk.

LINCOLN

There was a very nice '79 Mark V, Cartier edition, which I bought
at auction. Never having driven one before, I figured because it
was a high quality car, it would be a pleasure to drive. Well, it was
plush, but just plain too long. It required aiming rather than
driving. I sold it for less than half of what I paid, then got stiffed
for all of that. I couldn't believe the supposed friend did that to me,
especially when I was out of work. He drove it for years.

Obviously the car was a lot better than his word, which is really the
true measure of a person.

I have another Lincoln story, but it wasn't even my car. It was a 1957 and I took it to the Hershey, PA car show to sell for a friend, around 1974. I made it there, but the car developed electrical charging problems en route. It was a Saturday morning and the counter man at the parts store directed me to a building where an ace mechanic named Oline Light fixed cars. He opened the shop just for us. It was on the second floor of -- I think -- an old factory. He guided me onto an ancient elevator, and up we went. Then we drove about fifty yards to a corner section, and Oline proceeded to remove and rebuild the generator. Basically this meant he installed new brushes and cleaned the armature so the grooves were again grooves. He put it together and we were back in business.

Now comes the best part. I said, "How much?" and with a two-tooth smile, after emitting a goodly amount of tobacco juice, he replied, "Seven bucks'll do ya."

It kind of puts in perspective where this country has gone in forty years…from someone being able to make a living at $3.00/hr to money so devalued that our country adds twenty thousand bucks every second to our debt, and that's just the interest on what the US owes, mostly incurred through bureaucracy and waste. The economists and politicians a hundred years ago weren't too bad. The country was strong, respected, and we had no debt or taxes. How bad was that?

MERCURY

There was a 1949 two-door coupe which was one of several cars I bought from my good friend, Albin. In fact, as a side note, if anybody wanted to produce an Archie Bunker type sitcom, Al's garage would make many people wealthy. He is grumpy, but I'm sure it's a front because really he's a softy, and would help anybody in need. Back to the '49. It was James Dean relived, dual exhausts and overdrive. It had orange lights behind the grill and at night resembled a cut-out pumpkin with a lit candle inside. It developed a burnt valve and although it shouldn't have bothered me, as I had gone on a 9000-mile trip with the same problem a year earlier, I sold it to Parker for twenty-five bucks. When I was demonstrating how it could still burn rubber, I popped the clutch and ruined first gear. He bought it for $15 anyway.

That kid loved to have fun at almost any cost. I remember going down a big hill with his mother driving a 1950 Packard. Parker was in the back, I in the front, and all of a sudden he reached around his mother's head and covered her eyes. Imagine, she laughed and said, "He's such a devil!" Another time we were racing down the highway, him in front, when all of a sudden he stood up on the seat and mooned me. I wish a cop had seen him, and I wish I could have seen the arrest report. Whenever he rode on my motorcycle, he would sit backwards, then occasionally, he'd make the bike tip over as we went slow around a corner. I didn't laugh much then, but reflecting on those times always makes me smile, despite the bruises and road rash.

During the winter on snowy roads, we would take turns holding on to the back bumper, sitting on a Flexible Flyer sled, cruising the back roads. Once I remember hitting 50 mph. Fortunately the "man upstairs" always prevented a Darwin Award-winning final chapter, even though our IQs were up to the task.

Next, a 1977 Cougar XR7, solid, good-running, and one owner. I intended to paint it to obliterate the exterior themed Cougar artwork. After getting it home, I decided not to paint, because it was just too good to destroy, plus everybody liked it. So here's a picture, and if anybody is interested it's available for $4500, or thereabouts.

Next there was a 1987 Grand Marquis Colony Park eight-passenger wagon. It was an estate car, low miles, one owner, always garaged, all options including leather seats. It's really nice, and rides as well as the 1991 Fleetwood Brougham. It's even good on gas with its small V8, and electronic fuel injection. It has practicality plus class, and I'd rather have it than a minivan, any day.

Maybe the most interesting was a 1941 Mercury wagon that got crashed with only 9000 miles at the time of the accident. It was too good to junk, so a clever woodworker fashioned a body from oak and mahogany. The rocker panels were five inches thick. The chassis and running gear remained original. The very talented wood guy probably spent a thousand hours in its construction. I drove it only once. I didn't have the knowledge or money to finish the project. I swapped it and a good-running 1952 BMW motorcycle for a Karman Ghia and a decent 1961 190SL Mercedes.

These were all nice and very collectible items, but they were perfect examples of the notion that "nothing reduces the value of an item more than paying little or nothing for it." When I traded, I had about $550 into the BMW and the wooden car. I sold the good-running 190 SL for $400 and used the Karman Ghia for a year before driving it to the boneyard. Another example of the "

Reduced Value Phenomenon" happened when I gave my neighbor a 6x6 cedar post. Their mailbox and pole got damaged badly, I guess by a car or vandals, I don't know. Anyway, it was in sad condition and stayed that way for weeks and weeks. I could not have cared less about its looks, but I knew his wife liked the house to look nice. I decided to give them the post to use for the mailbox. It was not an easy decision, as I had gotten it from a job I was working on at the time. It was from a famous person's historic estate. I like stories attached to things, so I struggled a lot giving it away. His wife and daughter were gracious -- and, I think, grateful -- and thanked me. I guess the husband was working. Their knowing where it came from was immaterial, and so, unmentioned. About five or six weeks later, a new post and mailbox were installed. He probably tossed or gave the treasured post away, figuring I didn't want it anyway. I'll carry that memory to my grave.

OLDSMOBILE

First there was a 1942. It was a big car with a flathead six and an automatic transmission. Although I loved the way it rode and drove, it defined the word "slow." I couldn't go fast if I wanted, and I was fine with that. I sold it to Tar, as he wanted an old car. He in turn sold it to Teabags, who drove it for a while before selling it to its present owner. I occasionally see it on the road and at shows now, forty-eight years later, and very likely someday it will be back in my driveway.

Next, a 1988 Cutlass Supreme Classic, the last of an era. Production stopped at the end of 1988, and rear wheel drive Cutlasses ended. I bought it new, and it still looks nice, with no rust. It has factory wheels with bigger tires and Bilstein shocks. It sits just right. Son Rick has claim to it, and he deserves it, and lots more. Forget about our blood ties -- I'm privileged just to know him and his siblings. They are great people.

PACKARD

First I had a 1950. I swapped it for a custom-bodied Daimler convertible. Going back to Chevrolets, you might recall the hell trip to Chicago trying to deliver the Daimler. I was lucky to survive that one.Next there was a 1951. It was excellent -- see picture.

I drove it to an auction about a thousand miles away. A ring broke just before I got there. I left it at a garage for repair, then flew back home. I retrieved it three months later, to use in a niece's wedding. She lived in the same town where I had it repaired. Things do happen for a reason, and the next story reinforces that.

This story is about a 1954 Packard Clipper Super. I had seen it in a driveway over the course of several years, and it appeared not to move. I finally decided to stop, as I had time due to not having a job. The owner, an eighty-five-year-old gent, said it was a great car and very quiet. He was right: the handling, steering, and braking were amazing for a car that big and heavy. Packard's motto was "Just Ask the Man Who Owns One." Although it had gone only about 54,000 it was a bit shabby. My $70 offer was short, but with a rare stroke of creativity, I offered to paint his house for the car and $200. If you'd seen his house, you'd know why he jumped at the offer.

Of course he had no idea that I was clueless, and had never before lifted a paint brush. The house was peeling badly. I reasoned that even I could improve its looks. I got "how-to" info from the paint store and did the job. From eyesore to attractive home and seeing the owner smiling with pride -- that was special. It was so satisfying, in fact, that I put an ad in the local newspaper for paint work, and the calls haven't stopped. My work has run the gamut over the last forty five years, from the nastiest work to gilding the dome and weathervane at Yale's Pierson College. Like I said, things happen for a reason, and the Clipper Super was a life changer.

Another example was my buying land on eBay. Nutty as it sounds, it was a good deal and beautiful property. As a result of that purchase I became a good friend of, and business associate with, a jeweler turned custom cue stick maker/inventor. He's so talented, and his name is Chuck Starkey. He lives near my children's property in Warsaw, Missouri. If any of you readers are in the market for a special one-of-a-kind cue stick, Chuck is the man.

PLYMOUTH

First was a 1947 special deluxe convertible that I bought so cheap, it didn't bother me at all to swap it for two 1957 Dodge Lancer hubcaps. The new owner was my friend Jeanie's husband, and I have a gut feeling he was okay with the deal.

Next there was a 1951 Cranbrook two-door sedan. I remember going to my boss, Tar's father, and asking him for my pay because I wanted to buy a car. He said, "What the hell kind of car? I only owe you fifty-four bucks." That was plenty.

About the same time, a friend was home on leave waiting for his medical discharge papers from the Air Force. His base was in Kansas, about 1500 miles away. He also had an old car stored there. I thought it would be an adventure to drive him back to get discharged, then maybe buy an old car myself and return home in tandem. About three weeks later he was notified of his discharge and told to come back in order to finalize the paperwork. His base was one of Strategic Air Command, so in my attempt to fit the situation, and simulate an aircraft, I cut the '51 Cranbrook's steering wheel in half. Imagine, if you will, making a panicked left or right turn and grabbing nothing but air, instead of the steering wheel.

With the muffler scraping the road occasionally, off we went. Around 500 miles later it fell off, totally shot. A local parts store supplied a glasspack muffler and directions to a garage in a very, very back alley. Two colorful gentlemen named Hayes Haras and Bill Jaxon agreed to install the new muffler. About three hours, some ginger brandy, and a lot of laughs later, we were back on the road. We did reach Kansas, and although the car was good on gas, it used a case of oil in about 1500 miles. While there, after hitting a pole due to very heavy fog and poor visibility, I sold the car for $35. It still ran, and I think the buyer liked the half steering wheel. I then bought a 1937 Plymouth Coupe for $65, and we proceeded back to Connecticut in mid-January 1963, but not before I crashed my new acquisition.

I was turning left at a busy intersection and feeling good about having a whole steering wheel when, as fate would have it, a very attractive female was pumping gas nearby. I gazed too long and when my attention returned to driving, it was too late. All I saw were four very large wide eyes anticipating the unavoidable. They belonged to a black couple, she being about eight months pregnant. Luckily there were no apparent injuries, but their 1951 Lincoln was totaled.

If you recall, I was insurance-less, and now in deep trouble. After three or four days of waiting, we met again at the police station. What happened next was miraculous, and to this day I have no idea why the gentleman approached me and said, "I don't want to get into any trouble. Let's forget about the whole thing." I quietly got in my '37, which although smashed, was still drivable; I went to fetch my friend, and quickly departed for Connecticut.

Leaving quickly didn't mean driving quickly. It took four days nearly nonstop to go 1500 miles. Actually, the nearly nonstop staying awake part was easier for me than Dennis. His car, a 1935 Chevy coupe, which I had to drive because it had to be shifted at the proper engine rpm range and he couldn't master that, had no driver's side window. The air temperature averaged about 5 degrees Fahrenheit. I was much closer to freezing than to falling asleep. While the shifting was tricky, add the fact that I was in a sleeping bag from the waist down, trying to work the clutch, brake, and gas pedals. Those four days were pretty memorable and defined the phrase "trip from hell."

After being home a few months, I located a perfect grill and shell surround for the Plymouth. It was in a nearby junkyard. The mechanic removed the pieces from the donor car and had it sitting in his garage. Like I said, it was perfect, and the cost was $8! I did remove and replace the parts myself. The dented fenders were fixable and my friend, The Broomer, painted the coupe for $200. Wish I still had that one also. See pictures.

An ironic addendum to the Kansas accident occurred one year later as we were going through the same town on the return leg of our speed run to California. We were stopped for a traffic light at an intersection when a car, speeding around the corner, almost hit my old Buick. It was only inches away, on two wheels, when I caught a glimpse of his profile. I blurted "THAT'S HIM!" I turned around and followed him home. Sure enough, it was the man I had hit a year earlier. How random was that, and could anybody ever calculate the odds, if in fact he had hit me? We had a good laugh about the long shot coincidence; I'm just a little wary about going back to Salina, Kansas.

Then there was a1962 Fury race car: I was lucky to break even on that one, basically because racers are stuck on the two-door post car stigma. I had it at a show, and the only person who liked the car was a boy of about ten or eleven. I asked why he liked it and he replied, "Because it's a four-door." I love that kid! I sold it to a man who wanted only the drive train. Too bad -- it really was pretty cool, and fast! I also had a couple of early 1960s Fury wagons. They were well used, but still excellent to drive.

Next, a 1970 Cuda ragtop clone. It was born as a 318 Barracuda convertible, and then someone changed things a bit. The

motor was replaced with a high performance 440 magnum engine, and two more carburetors were added. Now essentially it became a v-code, or 440-6 car. 440 was the cubic inch displacement of the engine, and the 6 referred to triple 2 barrel carburetors, or as Plymouth badged it, a 6-barrel. Dodge's counterpart was titled a 6-pack car. Whatever the term, it was race car fun to drive. A best friend, Fitzgerald, will attest to that.

It was a good car to clone because in true factory form, only twenty-nine were made. They became desirable, and the investment was a good choice. I kept it for two years. Before it was sold, I gave my neighbor Dave, its previous owner, a month's labor painting his house. After it was sold I promised him that when his home needed painting again, I would do the job again if physically able, at no charge.

PONTIAC

I've had a '54 sedan, a pretty rare '55 standard shift station wagon, and my favorite, a '47 coupe. I loved its looks. My dad used it for two years. He hated to shift, so it was second and reverse, no matter where he went. Fortunately he never went more than six or seven miles in town. One night it got vandalized and all the windows were broken, with other miscellaneous damage -- a sad end to a great car. Lastly, I had a show- winning, 29,000 mile GTO 400 four-speed, which after five years I sold to help my son John start his career. That was the same son who had to use the VW the night it caught fire, and had to use my mint Silverado pickup to go about 500 miles, never checking the oil, which did

ruin the motor. One other tidbit about that son. He is a great father, husband, and Vice President of Product Design for the giant toy company,Hasbro, and yet finds the time to call his mom and I almost daily .

SUBURBANS

There were several, the first of which was wrecked by my second son, Rick, who at age fourteen decided to go for a joy ride. Without explaining the details, you may correctly imagine that was also costly for Papa. Not to exclude my third son from this group, he also was no stranger to causing Daddy and Mommy many sleepless nights, due to automotive indiscretions. Our daughter, on the other hand, was pretty good, I think. Other than begging me to let her take the station wagon to her junior prom, and crashing into a fence, she was conscientious…or just lucky. Even the fence thing was okay because of snowy conditions, and she was a new driver. You know, of course, it's *not* the "Daddy's Little Girl" phenomenon talking, don't you?

Back to Suburbans -- they just feel secure. I still use one for work. It's a two-wheel drive fuel injected 350, and fully loaded. It still gets 16 to 17 mpg on the highway. Whether the payload is equipment or people, it is cost efficient, despite what others may say.

MOTORCYCLES

I've had three BSAs, three Triumphs, two BMWs, two Suzukis, three Yamahas, and a brand-new Honda Valkyrie. That was an incredible machine and, I say, among the best motorcycles ever made. Alas, physical disabilities told me not to tempt fate, and it found a very happy new owner. But, for peace of mind, I still keep an old Yamaha XS Eleven, just to satisfy an occasional urge.

FOREIGN CARS

I've owned a couple of Mercedes. Besides the 190 SL I took in trade for the wood car, I had a 1958 model 180D. The D stood for diesel. My good and ever sarcastic friend Albin always and unaffectionately referred to it as "the staff car." See picture. I'll never forget Bobby Ruzzo's words the first time he saw it. "What fool would ever sell such a car!" He was right on the money except for one word, which should have been *buy* instead of sell. Although it had probably been good once, it really was junk!

There was one Saab, a three-cylinder model, I bought from my friend Paul, whose son Steve I went to school with. The Saab was quite a car, and an absolute departure from anything American in 1965. Since it had front wheel drive, I could scare my passengers when entering turns at twice the normal speed. A new experience, adrenaline with safety -- wow!

Next, a VW and regrettably -- but still worth mentioning -- I did not buy Linda's good-running 1951 VW for $25. Bring *that* day back!

Then there was a solid 1957 which I sold to a man who did a beautiful restoration during the next two years. I was happy it went to someone who authored its best chapter, I'm sure.

Next, a new 1968 for Sue, which was the first semi-automatic in town. She couldn't drive a standard, and I won't discuss the events that happened as a result of my trying to teach her. Believe me, they're better left unmentioned!

After that, there was a very memorable 1958 which I purchased from Mr. Davis, who I'm sure could triple the length of this book with his own vehicle entanglements. Anyway, after having it painted and a few things fixed, it looked and ran great, till one fateful evening. You remember…son John, a fire, no more car, and of course no fire insurance.

I had a new Special Edition Honda Accord in 1984. It was a nice car, but went through front brake pads so fast. The factory said it was normal for an automatic, front wheel drive, always in traffic, with a female driver (named Sue?). I sold it to friends Ely and Irene. It was for their daughter and it had a good, long life thereafter.

Next, a 1976 Civic wagon. It was another car I bought from my good friend Albin. I told him if my four children could sit across the back seat uncrowded, I would buy it. They did, and I did. I used it for many years. Once, after a 2500-mile trip, upon returning home the transmission gave out two blocks from my home. I got it repaired for reasonable money and drove it another 60,000 miles. The last couple of years it was used as a work vehicle, once carrying eighteen five-gallon containers of paint to a job forty miles away. It had a roof rack, so besides carrying over a half ton of paint, I had several ladders on top, including a forty-footer. I really wish I had a picture of that!

I went to Virginia once to paint Gormley's house with my friend and painting associate, Billy Bergeron. We got stuck in a tunnel because the Honda's cooling fan malfunctioned and the car overheated. Another memorable sight, unfortunately unphotographed, was pushing the little wagon, ladders atop it, through a long tunnel.

Rust caused its final demise, but not before it burned oil so bad when it started that if you just let it idle in place, the only thing visible was smoke, no car. Fun memories...even going to dinner fifty miles away with four adults and six children, pre-seatbelt era, of course. *That* was safe!

Although I'm not usually one to buy foreign cars, I must admit the 2006 purchase was a good one. Normally a new car purchase for me takes months due to product research, price shopping, etc. The following story was different.

One rainy Saturday evening while reading the paper in my pajamas, I spotted an interesting ad which read: "Buy a car at 9 p.m. and get a year's free gas." My next thought was *Where's my pants? I'm curious.* I got there at about 8:30 and was the only customer. They wanted to sell a car. I got a great deal on a Kia

Optima, and also for my trade-in car. Then a week or so later I received a check for a year's worth of gas. They calculated it to be $1320. Throw in Kia's ten-year 100,000 mile warranty and it was a no- brainer. It's a pleasure to drive, and after 90,000 miles it's still trouble-free.

Although Kia had a bad rap due to the inherent poor quality of a cheap car, Hyundai bought them in 1998 and really improved their product. It was good to learn that they contributed to the 911 Help Fund, a distinction that only one other foreign car maker can claim. I don't feel un-American owning the Kia, especially since I still own and drive six USA vehicles.

Next and last on the foreign scene was a 1980 Toyota Tercel, the only new car I ever bought without financing. Coming home late one Friday evening following our ritual weekly card game – a thirty-five year tradition -- I got a flat tire. I knew the spare was flat, as I never got it fixed following a previous flat tire incident. Rather than drive home on a flat, not uncommon for me, I pulled over. My good friend Albin was a passenger and I chose not to give him ammunition for future jokes at my expense. I knew another card player wasn't far behind, and flagged her over. She gave us a ride home and all was well, I thought. Next morning I went to fetch the car, but it was gone. I called the police to ask if they knew anything. They did and told me it was hit at about 2:00 a.m. I remember leaving the car with Al at 1:54 a.m. It had been hit right where I would have been changing the flat, if I'd had a good spare. I guess our time just wasn't up yet. Well, of course not; I had to write this book.

STUDEBAKER

I've owned a so-so 1960 truck and a 1941 car. The car was really good-looking but needed a motor. I found a supposed new engine from an old Studebaker dealership. I bought and installed it, but while turning it over by hand I could hear a rod knock. Being discouraged after all that work, I sold it. Too bad; it was perfect for a street rod.

Next, a 1947 one and a half ton stake body truck that was restored and mint. I gave $200 and a 1929 International pickup with a hand crank starter that ran great. The Studebaker was too big for my garage and too nice to leave outside. Dan Roberts loaned me his big International Loadstar flatbed. I loaded the Stude on the back and left for Hershey, PA in hopes of selling both vehicles. Although the trucks didn't sell, I was really happy to avoid a tragedy in the making. En route, about 1:00 a.m., while I was lost somewhere in rural Pennsylvania, the Loadstar brakes went out. I coasted to a stop. Nothing was open, but I had just passed a large open lot. I backed up, rolling to a stop in the lot, figuring I would rest and try to find a mechanic at daybreak. A witness to this, and many other stories, was Marty, my good friend and business partner of thirty years. He was following in my New Yorker wagon, which doubled as emergency vehicle/sleeping quarters. We got up around 6:00 a.m., got out to survey the area, and EUREKA! We were at the far end of an International truck dealership. It was at least a million to one shot at the perfect moment in time. Things like that just don't happen by chance.

The dealership opened at 7:00 and we were back on the road by 7:45 with a new brake line replacing an illegal copper line someone installed, which finally split. That great picture of my red and black fendered Studebaker atop the red and black fendered International doing 70 mph down the interstate could easily have become a large pile of mangled metal. How nice that it didn't.

There was a 1940 Studebaker I did not buy because of the transmission being apart. I wish I had, just for the story of its life till then. It was bought new by my neighbor, and was his first and only car ever. I think that was really special, and so against today's society -- which brings this book to its final chapter, about a 1941

Packard which has survived untouched and been a constant in my family for the last fifty years.

OUR 1941 PACKARD CLIPPER

I'm privileged and enjoy being part of a tiny and dwindling group of people who obtained pre-war cars from their first owners. The historical significance of this Packard is further enhanced by its near mint, original, and unrestored condition. With many, many shows, weddings, and even a funeral, my experiences with it could be a book by itself. In fact, it was the subject of a yet unpublished children's book I wrote back in the '70s. I tried to convey the value of taking care of things and machines so they would last a long time. Hopefully this in turn would generalize to saving and protecting good friendships and relationships. In short, throw away the "Throw Away Society."

Although I appear guilty of major consumerism due to the number of cars, trucks, and motorcycles I've owned, I tend more to just enjoy and appreciate the genius of designers and engineers. Every vehicle has a story, and hopefully its time with me adds a good chapter. The following is a reprinted article on the above mentioned Packard, courtesy of the MERIDEN-RECORD JOURNAL newspaper written by Jeffery Kurz:

MERIDEN – At least one automobile in Rick Reale's driveway isn't going to do him any favors should gas prices reach the $4-a-gallon mark this summer, but this car has value that goes way beyond the scope of mere transportation.

Reale is the second owner ever of his 1941 Packard Clipper, a storied automobile manufactured by a storied car company. The Clipper was one of just 10 of its kind sold by Meriden's Scanlon dealership that year. It sold to postman Frank Mellon on May 5, about seven months before the attack on Pearl Harbor. Packard, always a renowned maker of engines, would turn efforts toward making aircraft engines for the war effort.

" Being the second owner of a '41 Packard is extremely rare" said Ron Eastwood, former president of the Eastern Packard Club, based in Stratford.

Reale's Packard has never been refurbished and remains in pristine condition. The engine still runs with satisfying smoothness. When Reale changed the oil last year for the first time in 20 years, it was still clear.

The odometer reads 60,205.5. Reale has put just about 16,000 miles on the car since he bought it in 1967. Because it remains as showy and prestigious as the day it left the lot, Reale uses it to escort family members to weddings. He's also been taking it to classic auto shows, where it's been earning trophies.

The car, which sports Packard's "flying lady" hood ornament, was first in its class last year, for "untouched originals" at a show in Bridgehampton, N.Y., for example. An award in August, at the

41st annual Easthampton Car Show, coincided with Reale and his wife,Sue, celebrating their 41st year of marriage.

"It's a gorgeous car", said John Peterson, an 88 year old collector from East Hampton who has bought and sold about 100 Packards and still owns three.

" You don't see too many of that model," said Peterson. " He's kept tremendous care of it. It's still like new."

The rich history of American auto manufacturing is still evident on the nations roadways and at classic car events. It's not unusual for classic cars to be in original condition, said Steven Moskowitz, executive director of the Antique Auto Club of America, which, with about 61,000 members, is the largest club of it's kind in the U.S.

"There are a lot of original cars out there and a lot of owners like to keep them that way," said Moskowitz. " Any time you have a car that is completely original and a half-century old, that's pretty cool."

John Scanlon, who died in 1956, was 17- year postmaster appointed by U.S. senator Francis T. Maloney in 1936. Since 1923, Scanlon had run a dealership that sold Packard and DeSoto cars.

The 1941 Clipper was a new model for Packard with a new chassis that allowed the car to sit lower. Packard made 16,00 of that model, said Reale.

When postal service worker Frank Mellon bought his Packard he was given a postal employee discount. Reale still has the records from the deal, jottings on the cover of a sales brochure.

Mellons discount was $76.75, which brought the price of the car to $1,459.25. He had to pay $59.50 for a radio and $28.35 for a heater. The selling price was $1,546.85. While cheap by today's standards, it was pricey for the time. Packards were elite cars. The company's slogan was " Ask the man who owns one ."

"Packards were renowned for being sturdy and elegant," Eastwood said.

Reale, who turns 64 in a couple of weeks is just a few years younger than his automobile. He's a member of the 1962 Platt High Sscool class, the first to go through all four years at the school. Reale, an independent painting contractor, says he has always liked classic cars, and started looking around for one to buy while he was in college.

He bought the Packard from Mellon in 1967, for $600.00. Today its worth is hard to gauge, though Reale says the value has been rising in recent years because of the enthusiasm of collectors. He's not adverse to selling it under the right circumstances.

" I'd like to see it in a museum," he said. " I think it deserves that."

The automobile has no seat belts, but does come with cigar lighter, map light, a clock on the glove compartment face and an interesting feature that might take a little of the sting out of climbing gas prices. The car emits a whistling noise as you pump, with the tone changing to signal a filling tank. Incidentially, the price of gas in 1941 was less than 20 cents.

Below is a great illustration done by John Packard Reale symbolizing two great American loves, BASEBALL and CARS.

I hope this little book has caused smiles and rattled memories. I'm sure many readers will even say, Heck, I could easily write a book about vehicle experiences. So although my story is over for now, I'll be looking for YOURS !

Comments invited and should be sent to rickreale@yahoo.com

Made in the
USA
Middletown, DE